MW01242145

Wait! Don't Throw In The Towel

Lateena Pettis

Edited By: Denise O'Neill

DEDICATION

I am dedicating this book to my husband, my king, and my headship. This booked was birthed because of the love that we share for one another. Through the trials, test, sufferings and adversities we have faced we have received an honor from God in an early stage of our marriage that most will never experience before they depart from this earth, let alone through a marriage. I am honored to share my life with you, I pray that we continue to be an example for generations to come, and that through God all things are possible. May God continue to bless each year of our covenant, and we live out and honor his word concerning the truth of the marital covenant. I will forever keep my covenant with you until God calls me home.
Loving You Always and Forever,
KOONTA

I thank God for such a bunch of understanding children who have purpose and vision and have supported all the work and time I have but into this book! May God continue to equip me to impart purpose, destiny and vision to each and every one of them!

Leadership Appreciation

I thank God who is the head of my life and I thank all who have equipped, trained, held me accountable and prayed me to this point in my process. Special appreciation to Pastor Lizzie Toomer (New Covenant Kingdom Ministries), Apostle Kevin Bailey (Touch of the Master Healing International Ministry), Apostle Taquetta Baker (Kingdom Shifters Ministries) Prophetess Tanya Wormley (Mashiach Ministries) it takes the body of Christ to pursue vision and I'm blessed to have you all!

Special Thanks

Special thanks to Tally Anderson (Hadassah Kingdom Ministries) for sisterhood & Devante Lamont (Renewed) for being a brother in the Kingdom. Also many thanks to Denise and Tom O'Neill for editing this book and being a blessing to the vision.
And importantly all family and friends that supported and believed in me there are too many to name but I love and thank all of you!

To Our Parents

Without our parents we wouldn't even be here! I'm so blessed to have four wonder people who I call mothers and fathers! God bless all of you and may God continue bless your covenants and the legacy that you have been allowed to leave for all the generations after you. Thank you for leading us to Jesus and teaching us the way to go!

CONTENTS

ACKNOWLEDGMENTS

"Lateena is a passionate person who can draw from a lot of her own life experiences to understand and empathize with people. She has overcome several difficult situations in her life which I feel gives her a great advantage to understanding the shortcomings of others. She cares deeply for people and I believe she has a skill set to teach and guide people through their life situations and struggles. Being a mother of 5 children ranging from age 3 to 17 also gives her a perspective that not many can relate to. Anyone lucky enough to work with her child or adult will benefit life long."
Stephanie Flannery —colleague and friend

"Lateena's words in this book have been led by Christ and have truly penetrated our hearts in a profound way. Her love for God and how He's changed her marital life speaks volumes. What my husband and I have learned through our marriage is that when we have a closer more personal relationship with God, we have a deeper, more passionate love for one another. When He is at the center of our 3-strands strong, we are not easily broken: God, husband, and wife. Every season of our lives together brings new challenges that could make or break us, but it's through only our Lord Jesus Christ that we have strength to face and overcome with renewed direction. Tom professes to put God first, and each other's needs above your own. All glory and praise to God bringing and keeping us together!"
~ Tom and Denise O'Neill

Declaration

I pray that as you read this book that your eyes are
opened to biblical covenant and that you receive the
grace and faith to have a marriage founded on
Jesus. I declare that healing and forgiveness is
released and hearts are mended. I declare that those
not married are equipped to understand the
assignment of marriage. I declare that each reader
receives the double favor, honor, and blessing that
is received through obedience and sacrifice. I
declare that each reader receives specific
instructions and strategey concerning their own
marriages and families. I pray that peace and joy be
your portion and each family be protected and
covered by the blood in Jesus Name

Amen

FOUNDATION OF COVENANT

For When God made a promise to Abraham, because he could swear by no greater, he swore by himself. Hebrews 6:14

From the beginning of time God has promised us covenant through Abraham and it still stands today. There are many examples of covenant promises between God and man throughout the scripture. God never broke his covenant with man, but there are many times man breaks covenant with God.   Although this covenant was breeched by man, God still remained faithful and kept the promise.

What does the bible say about marriage and the covenant? According to:

Malicah 2:14-16 it says *14 Yet you say, "For what reason?" Because the Lord has been witness between you and the wife of your youth, with whom you have dealt treacherously; yet she is your companion and your wife by covenant. 15 But did He not make them one, having a remnant of the Spirit? And why one? He seeks Godly offspring. Therefore, take heed to your spirit, and let none deal treacherously with the wife of his youth. 16 "For the Lord God of Israel says That He hates divorce, for it covers one's garment with violence," Says the Lord of hosts. "Therefore take heed to your spirit, that you do not deal treacherously."*

This scripture is a picture of infidelity where God describes marriage as a holy institution. In this particular passage it speaks of men committing adultery. I do not believe that God is bias and picking on men, but in the times of the bible headship was taken seriously and the man was the leader and authority in the relationship. Nowadays people are getting married for opportunity and for show. They are not taking the institution of marriage seriously and do not have the revelation or wisdom to last in one. This is why we see so many marriages dissolving before year five and sometime by year two. There is an ever present holiness attached to the covenant of marriage and the union is closing, binding and pure. I used the passage in Malachi to allow you to understand that although infidelity is such a betrayal of trust and exposes disloyalty and lack of confidence in God and in self, a marriage even in this state is not beyond restoration. I believe that infidelity is probably the most damaging things that can be done against your marriage aside from physical abuse. I do not advocate physical abuse or the threat of your life. If you are being abused physically, please seek help immediately.

Because a marriage is considered holy in the sight of God, it is on the priority list of the enemy to destroy, so that the institution of family may be destroyed along with it. This happened in the beginning when Eve was tempted by satan in the garden to eat of the forbidden tree. What deception is being sent your way at this moment in your marriage that you would consider divorce and not restoration?

Genesis 3:1 Now the serpent was more cunning than any beast of the field which the Lord God had made. And he said to the woman, "Has God indeed said, 'You shall not eat of every tree of the garden'?"

God created marriage between man and woman to become one flesh through a lifetime process and to produce Godly children within the union. Becoming one does not happen instantly at the wedding once vows are quoted. When your marriage is deemed holy in the sight of God, your seed is blessed and makes it easier to train up a child in the way of God so that the legacy of truth continues to be the foundation of the earth until the return of Jesus. Why did I say that it is easier this way? I have not been a perfect parent nor have I raised my children in the way that I should the entire time, but when I yielded to the word and started to live it instead of preaching it, I became a model of the word instead of it being forced. My children wanted to know more and I was now equipped to give them what they needed. I had to be in right standing with God to even be an example to my children. This made me want to dig even deeper into marriage and model these roles as well.

After learning about why God created such a covenant and the foundation that it should be built on, I found it very difficult to just throw in a towel and walk away, even though I was tempted by my feelings and emotions to throw it all away, my faith was weak and built on fallow ground. If Jesus lives in you, then his words live through you and faith shouldn't allow for you to just give up.

I found that I had so many past hurts and adversities that were blocking my right to have a Godly covenant. There was much healing and deliverance needed and instead of yielding, I was putting expectations on my husband that weren't even his responsibility. For example, I would repeatedly say you do not make me happy. Then one day the Holy Spirit said he is not supposed to make you happy. Happiness, joy and peace come from the father in heaven. Honestly, when I heard that I was like, "Dang I can't blame him anymore," and I immediately felt convicted. I kept thinking about how many times I had told him he didn't make me happy and how he must have felt when I released that over him. It was at this moment that I decided enough was enough, I wasn't going to throw in the towel, I was going to fight for my marriage, and this book was birthed through pain, trials, test and faith! Even though I have only been married nine years, I thank God that I have suffered and preserved through it to impart keys to other young married couples to be offensively fighting in the war with hell over your covenant. If you are not married yet or you are already in a raging war if you are already married I am a witness that it can be restored. Marriage is war, and if you are married and don't agree then you may want to check and see what foundation your marriage is built on. My marriage was built on flesh and emotionalism. We honestly loved each other and wanted the best, but we blindly went in to covenant unprepared. And when those vows were released and we were on our way to becoming one, all hell broke loose and we had no keys, wisdom, faith or strategy on how to fight for it. It was like being thrown into a boxing match with no gloves on. We still had to fight, but instead of fighting the real enemy we fought each other. We were blind and had not one weapon. We were bound, cursed and dying spiritually and so was our marriage. Neither one of us had a clue what to do, so it seemed hopeless. This is true for many today. There is no hope, and they would rather throw in the towel and be defeated than walk in the fullness of the covenant that God promised for marriage between man and wife.

I believe that as our relationships grow deeper with Jesus, that we go from glory to glory. I believe that as we go deeper into the process of marriage and bare the weight of the sacrifice, suffering, time, and energy that comes with it, we too will enter into different realms of marriage over the years.

Before I was healed, delivered and set free and understood the revelation for marriage, marriage was almost always a struggle for me, it seemed that even when I was getting the word and having a relationship with Jesus I still found myself alone and unfulfilled in my marriage. I begin to pray and desperately seek God on why I was feeling this way and it was simple ~ our marriage was not founded on Jesus. I didn't understand how this could be when we both believed in Jesus. But our beliefs were just a belief but we didn't live the word or even know the word. Our marriage began to have increased attacks after our first year and neither one of us had a clue how to fix or repair it. We were lost and although we loved each other and wanted to keep going, it seemed all hope was lost and it was easier to throw in the towel and give up, but we didn't.

We kept going and there was even a time of separation and trial but we didn't give up. There was even a time that divorce papers were drawn up, but we didn't give in. There was something in the both of us fighting for us when we didn't know how to fight for ourselves.

Jeremiah 1:19 They will fight against you, But they shall not prevail against you. For I am with you," says the Lord, "to deliver you.

There was definitely a war and neither my husband nor I had any idea what was going on. There was so much damage and confusion, I knew the Lord was keeping us but all I had was blind faith with no vision. There was a time that we were separated and lived apart and this is when God started to deal with me alone. I was introduced to deliverance for the first time and was given a prophetic word. My first thought was this is crazy, they are actually casting demons out of me and this is real! It was not only real; it was life changing. I begin to seek God for answers concerning so many things and I begin to be hungry for the word like never before and I began to want my marriage back. Although I wanted it back, I didn't know how it would be because I knew some truth but my husband did not. I was like how is this going to work God, he wanted me back home and does not want to end the marriage, but I really didn't know how to tell him that, I had some demons cast out of me. It was all new but I stepped out on faith and we moved back in together.

A few months after I moved back we started attending church together, it was a start, but all I could think about was my freedom, the deliverance and I wanted so much of Jesus. Eventually I was attending service alone and my husband's momentum for the word was gone. I felt so defeated. This is when I received my first vision for my marriage, it is this vision that has pushed me to not throw in the towel and give up on my covenant. It is with this vision that I'm able to write this book and it is this vision that my marriage will continue to thrive, honor and give glory to God.

Genesis 15:1 After these things the word of the Lord came to Abram in a vision, saying, "Do not be afraid, Abram. I am your shield, your exceedingly great reward

This scripture tells me that Abraham saw a vision of words that read do not be afraid and they appeared to him. One Sunday during worship I begin to weep, because I was so lonely, I was attending service Sunday after Sunday alone or with just my kids. As a year approached, I begin to feel defeated. It was this particular service that I just came in heavy and overwhelmed with hurt, rejection and abandonment. While I sat in my chair and looked up, I saw my husband in chains and he was chained to a wall. But when I looked again, I saw him pulling the chains out of the wall and then he embraced me and I held him in my breast. The Lord spoke to me and said no matter what happens, stand. No matter what anybody tells you to do, stand, and no matter how hard it gets, stand.

Genesis 15:15-18 ¹⁵ Now as for you, you shall go to your fathers in peace; you shall be buried at a good old age. ¹⁶ But in the fourth generation they shall return here, for the iniquity of the Amorites is not yet complete."

¹⁷ And it came to pass, when the sun went down and it was dark, that behold, there appeared a smoking oven and a burning torch that passed between those pieces. ¹⁸ On the same day the Lord made a covenant with Abram, saying:

"To your descendants I have given this land, from the river of Egypt to the great river, the River Euphrates

I believe that this vision was a promise to my husband and I that we were generational cycle breakers and that our covenant was forming a new bloodline a new breed a new way, just like when baby Isaac was born because God was birthing a new nation through Sarah and Abraham. Right after I received this vision, I found out I was pregnant with my youngest son he was born 7-14-14! Glory to God! Seven stands for wholeness and completeness and because our son was born on the seventh month on the 14 day that is a double portion and the birth year being 2014 confirms it. A NEW BLOODLIN ESTABLISHED GENERATIONAL CURSES BROKEN!!!! So you see it didn't' happen overnight. Over the last three years, I have had to fight, pray, fast, give grace and hang on to the vision and promise from God and stand immovable in my faith to stay in covenant. For without it, I would have thrown in the towel.

I believe God protected us although we didn't know we were carrying a purpose, a vision, or a destiny and God did not allow us to break covenant. This book was part of the reason why our covenant was not allowed to be breeched!

Glory to God!!!!!

YOU CAN'T THROW IN THE TOWEL

I can do all things through Jesus that strengthens me Philippians 4:13

Throwing in the towel in marriage is saying I'm tired, I can't do this anymore, I'm not happy, and this is not fulfilling. But marriage is not solely about you or just your happiness or your needs. When you come in agreement with divorce you are committing a sin and falling out of alignment with God and saying that you no longer trust the word. Divorce causes division, strife, difficulty and damage not only to the husband and wife but the institution of family in general. The word of God clearly states if you marry you will have trouble.

1 Corinthians 7:28 But even if you do marry, you have not sinned; and if a virgin marries, she has not sinned. Nevertheless, such will have trouble in the flesh, but I would spare you.

God was already warning us concerning marriage and the difficulties that we would face and the fight of the flesh that we have to overcome and be delivered from to understand the real fight is against spiritual powers, principalities, and the rulers of darkness that we cannot see.

Ephesians 6:12 12 For we do not wrestle against flesh and blood, but against principalities, against powers, against the rulers of the darkness of this age against spiritual hosts of wickedness in the heavenly places.

When you look at it like this, God was showing us that it is much easier to just please him than to be responsible for the affairs of another. Marriage is selfless and not about you and you have to understand that "I" statements cannot be a reason to throw in the towel. Divorce is a sin no matter how you try to dress it up, it is betrayal and a sin against each person involved husband and wife, and a sin according to the word of God. No matter who you think may or may not be at fault.

If you are considering throwing in the towel, then you have probably asked yourself how can you get a divorce and not be out of the will of God?   And why would divorce be permissible if it is considered a sin?

I believe that most of us have asked and pondered if divorce is a sin, then why is it permissible in the new testament?

Deuteronomy 24: 1-4 "When a man takes a wife and marries her, and it happens that she finds no favor in his eyes because he has found some uncleanness in her, and he writes her a certificate of divorce, puts it in her hand, and sends her out of his house ² when she has departed from his house, and goes and becomes another man's wife, ³ if the latter husband detests her and writes her a certificate of divorce, puts it in her hand, and sends her out of his house, or if the latter husband dies who took her as his wife, ⁴ then her former husband who divorced her must not take her back to be his wife after she has been defiled; for that is an abomination before the Lord, and you shall not bring sin on the land which the Lord your God is giving you as an inheritance.

In the old testament this is the picture of what marriage and divorce looks like today. You don't like your spouse, divorce them and get a new one, just don't go back to the one you left or who left you because that is considered an abomination before the Lord. Bringing sin on the family bloodline and placing curses on blessings that are promised to you. That does not seem fair at all but this is what the word is telling us. But the truth is you still should not get a divorce out of your own consensus. Jesus came to fulfill the law so we must see how this lines up with scripture in the new testament. Based on this particular scripture alone, you are permitted to divorce your spouse as long as you don't take them back and as long as you find them unclean or not in covenant with God in your sight. So this gives us permission not only to leave our spouse if they cheat, but we can also leave them if they are not in right standing with God. If this applies today, why would God give me a vision to stay and forbid me to leave my husband, this scripture alone permits both my spouse and I to throw in the towel.

Jeremiah 3:1 "They say, 'If a man divorces his wife, and she goes from him and becomes another man's, may he return to her again?' Would not that land be greatly polluted? But you have played the harlot with many lovers; Yet return to Me," says the Lord.

Now we are in Jeremiah and the scripture shows that the Lord is speaking even of the covenant we have with him and how we break covenant and then we are allowed to return. When the Lords speak of playing the harlot with many lovers, he is speaking of idolatry and putting other Gods before him. I call this committing spiritual adultery, but he gives grace and mercy, forgives and allows us to return back. So before Jesus even hit the scene, there was a lot of divorcing and adultery taking place in the natural and in the realm of the spirit in the old testament.

Matthew 5:31-32 ³¹ "Furthermore it has been said, 'Whoever divorces his wife, let him give her a certificate of divorce.' ³² But I say to you that whoever divorces his wife for any reason except sexual immorality[a] causes her to commit adultery; and whoever marries a woman who is divorced commits adultery.

Matthew 19:3-8. ³ The Pharisees also came to Him, testing Him, and saying to Him, "Is it lawful for a man to divorce his wife for just any reason?"

⁴ And He answered and said to them, "Have you not read that He who made[a] them at the beginning 'made them male and female,'[b] ⁵ and said, 'For this reason a man shall leave his father and mother and be joined to his wife, and the two shall become one flesh'?[c] ⁶ So then, they are no longer two but one flesh. Therefore, what God has joined together, let not man separate."

14

[7]They said to Him, "Why then did Moses command to give a certificate of divorce, and to put her away?"

[8]He said to them, "Moses, because of the hardness of your hearts, permitted you to divorce your wives, but from the beginning it was not so. [9]And I say to you, whoever divorces his wife, except for sexual immorality, [a] and marries another, commits adultery; and whoever marries her who is divorced commits adultery."

These particular scriptures always made me feel like I wasn't going to make it in my present marriage, because I, like many others, have been previously married. Both myself and husband of my previous marriage committed adultery. I committed adultery first and released what I had done to him, he forgave me and we picked up the pieces and moved on. This took place in the first six months of marriage. I was young and clueless and had no idea what marriage was, but we made it work. It was in the third year that it was exposed he was cheating on me. This pain was unbearable but because he forgave me three years prior, I wanted to forgive him and give him the same chance to make it right and restore. Although I wanted to fight, I was forced to get a divorce. Meaning I was served papers with no choice but to sign, my headship was stolen. I was so out of tune with the foundation of marriage that my husband was not only cheating but had fallen in love with another woman, divorced me and took her as his wife. We were defeated and my headship had thrown in the towel. I was so confused , I thought the bible would not allow me to be married again , I would read the scripture over and over again thinking I was doing something wrong and all along I was just being deceived by the enemy because I didn't understand that we were not longer under the old law. This is why it is important to not just go to church, but be the church and study the word of God for yourself. I the entire time being depressed and thinking if I ever married again that God wouldn't bless the union because my husband did not divorce me because I cheated. Well joke was on me and my deceived mind because we did actually divorce because of adultery but it was his betrayal that led to divorce along with a number of other reasons that we both shared equal blame for much of it being that we were not ready or equipped to be married.

I believe that Moses granted divorce as an option in the old testament because of the hardness, bitterness, rejection and roots of abandonment that could spring forth and take root in the heart and the damage would have been even greater if a divorce was not permissible. We see it all the time. People committing murder and suicide because of infidelity. Although it was permitted, it was still labeled a sin. Just because God gave free will to do it didn't change the fact that it was a sin.

The new testament in *Matthew* says that we should not depart from each other, but if we do we should remain unmarried or be reconciled. This sounds so unfair, but it was not a punishment but a blessing in disguise, although it gave me a feeling of hopelessness and being lost when my current husband and I separated when I got the revelation of this word it all became clearer what God was wanting to do and that it places his hand on the marriage. I believe that God did this to allow for reconciliation, forgiveness, repentance and restoration of the marriage covenants. How many times have you broke covenant with God and was allowed back? How many marriages have you heard being restored after infidelity, divorced but later they are remarried again? It is God that brings the marriage back together again. Our natural marriages are designed to function just as the function of the bride/bridegroom of the church. A threefold cord is not quickly broken.

Ecclesiastes 4:12

Though another may overpower one, two can withstand him. And a threefold cord is not quickly broken

1 Corinthians 7: 10-16¹⁰ Now to the married I command, yet not I but the Lord: A wife is not to depart from her husband. ¹¹ But even if she does depart, let her remain unmarried or be reconciled to her husband. And a husband is not to divorce his wife.

¹² But to the rest I, not the Lord, say: If any brother has a wife who does not believe, and she is willing to live with him, let him not divorce her. ¹³ And a woman who has a husband who does not believe, if he is willing to live with her, let her not divorce him. ¹⁴ For the unbelieving husband is sanctified by the wife, and the unbelieving wife is sanctified by the husband; otherwise your children would be unclean, but now they are holy. ¹⁵ But if the unbeliever departs, let him depart; a brother or a sister is not under bondage in such cases. But God has called us to peace. ¹⁶ For how do you know, O wife, whether you will save your husband? Or how do you know, O husband, whether you will save your wife?

I love this passage of scripture, but I believe that it is so misunderstood. In verse ten and eleven it clearly states divorce is not permitted and further states that even if we have a believing spouse with an unbelieving partner, we aren't permitted to leave. But if the unbelieving spouse leaves on their own accord, then it is permitted.

Now the problem that I see with this scripture is that people are getting healed, delivered and set free and then feeling like they unequally yoked with their spouse so they can leave. This is just not the case; it says they have to leave. Meaning you can't persuade them, you can't preach them out, and you can't cast them out! They have to leave on their own. I repeat, *"ON THEIR OWN ACCORD!"*

This can be super challenging for many, but it can be done. I have spent the last three years walking out my deliverance and believing for my spouse's breakthrough while going through some very difficult situations that many would have walked away from. But I learned so much about him and over time as I listened to the Holy Spirit, I forgot that he wasn't speaking in tongues, and laying hands on me, or reading scripture with me or doing all the things that people feel two bible-believing people should be doing and I just loved him where he was at. I'm not ashamed of my husband and I'm confidently speaking of him as my king and the headship of our family. When you obey the word of God and stay completely led by the spirit, there are secret keys that God reveals to you about your spouse. These keys can sometimes be deep rooted pain or hurt, or even the veil that they are wearing that is keeping them from breaking all the way through. I received many strategies on how to pray and cover my husband and my family, and I learned to respect that Gods timing is not always our timing. I learned that my husband has a journey with Jesus, just like I do and who am I to be all up in the relationship, my husband's relationship is private and intimate with Jesus, but he does have one and bears good fruit from it. I had to realize that I was not the perfect saint and I still needed grace daily myself so who was I to tell him how to have his relationship with Jesus.

I charge you to really stop and think about all I have released thus far in this book and reconsider throwing in the towel. God is a living; breathing, miracle-working God and the family structure is the will of God for our lives. This allows for alignment with Gods plan for marriage and family. Having faith and staying immovable in your earthly covenant will send total chaos and confusion to the enemy 's kingdom. It is my intention to deliberately push you into prayer and seeking vision and purpose for yourself and your marriage.

PRAYER

Father I thank you for each and every person who has sown a seed into their marriage by purchasing this book to gain insight and strategy on how to manifest reconciliation through faith, love, and grace. Lord I ask that you give each reader even the measure of grace that you have given me to push through and stand immovable for the sake of covenant. Grant each person a new measure of love and hope and cancel every scheme, plot, or device released upon him or her for seeking ways to restore instead of demolishing their covenant. I decree that even as you read the passages in this book you are becoming in tune with your spouse. I cancel all assignments of procrastination and lack of faith now in the name of Jesus and I call forth healing, deliverance and reconciliation in Jesus name. I pray that even the ones who are separated as one reads this book that the absence spouse will bear witness to the unction of the Holy Spirit. It is the will of God for you to be affluent in your marriage here on earth.

In Jesus name Amen

RECONCILIATION

2 Corinthians 5:18
18 Now all things are of God, who has reconciled us to Himself through Jesus Christ, and has given us the ministry of reconciliation,

As a believer we have been given the ministry of reconciliation and have been called forth to restore marriages and relationships that contain trust and covenants between people. Sometimes when we are considering restoring our marriages our emotions are all over the place and we go back and forth creating a doorway for fear, timidity and hopelessness to creep into our mind taking us into a soulish realm full of doubt and negative emotions. When we are in this soulish realm we begin to we ask ourselves a lot of questions like:

Did God really ordain this? Where did I mess up?

Is it my fault? What if there is too much damage?

There are many more questions that cross your mind, but I have discovered that if you can answer yes to the question below than you are on your way to restoration, healing and stability in your marriage.

Can I own what part my actions have played to get my marriage in such a place of turmoil?

You must understand that when you violate your covenant, you are putting your marriage and family in the risk of being out of alignment with the purposes and plans that are ordained for your marriage and family. The enemy is watching and waiting for an opportunity to come and cause division, strife, confusion and chaos and make you think it's you.

Jeremiah 29:11

11 For I know the thoughts that I think toward you, says the Lord, thoughts of peace and not of evil, to give you a future and a hope

1 Peter 5:8

Be sober, be vigilant; because your adversary the devil walks about like a roaring lion, seeking whom he may devour

We have to be careful even how we portray ourselves in the public eye especially when we are claiming to be followers of truth. Showing outwardly to appear to have it all together but behind doors dying away and suffering in vain. It is deception to think that God is honoring our worship and we are sinning against our spouses. This doesn't mean that we tell all our marital business or share intimate details but it may be that you need to step down from what you are doing and tend to your covenant. I remember a time when I was going through some extensive training in ministry and it took a lot of my focus from my marriage and family. I was always doing something for ministry whether I was on conference calls, traveling, taking equipping classes or just attending services. My husband would complain that I was always gone and I could sense he wanted me home more, but I was hungry for God and wanted to learn all that I could and felt like if he was on the same page as I was with his spirituality then things would be better and that was on him. I felt that is was not my fault that I wasn't home because if he wanted to spend time with me he would attend some of these services with me. I was so wrong about all of it and was going to learn the hard way, and all the worship, praying and fasting I was doing was in vain. Although my husband made many attempts to get me to devote more time at home with him and the kids, the more he pressed it, the further it drove me into ministry. It had been a year and I had completed my training and I was about to start another one that would take another year, but during the first month, it became more difficult for me to get to equipping class, my kids would be sick or my husband would have to work. You were only allowed to miss two classes and I had already missed two. I should have prayed and ask God to show me what was going on, but all I thought was this is an attack and the enemy was trying to stop me from gaining truth and training. I was deceived because I was allowing the enemy to come right on into my life and marriage because I was outside the will of covenant. My husband was the head and I was deliberately doing what I wanted and not even asking or praying to God about it. I was engaging in what I thought was spiritual warfare and basically fighting against myself. I was drained physically, emotionally and mentally. I spoke with my leader at the time and was advised to go to prayer and seek God for understanding, so I did. The following week it was exposed that my husband was reaching out to another woman for emotional support.

It was not completely clear at the time but I allowed this to happen. I wasn't being a wife at all and barely being a mother. I was not properly balancing all of this and because of that my husband was not getting his needs met emotionally, physically, or mentally from his wife. He was so mentally gone from the relationship that after it was exposed he was not sure about our marriage. This is when I had to really pray, and seek God alone for my next move. I had been advised for a year and listening to someone else tell me how God works but I didn't want to hear it anymore I wanted to just get it directly from God myself. I wanted to throw in the towel and just let it go. I was tired of the strain, drain and confusion. But surprisingly I was convicted in my spirit although my husband did his part I had played a role in it by not meeting the standard of a wife in our marriage.

I didn't speak to my husband for almost two weeks, but I did not leave. I was reminded of the vision and the promise and the instructions that no matter how hard it got I could not leave. I was torn but I had tools and I knew how to engage in spiritual warfare, I knew how to pray but instead of praying in vain this time I prayed thy will be done not my will be done.

Matthew 15:9

And in vain they worship Me, Teaching as doctrines the commandments of men

1 Peter 3:7

7 Husbands, likewise, dwell with them with understanding, giving honor to the wife, as to the weaker vessel, and as being heirs together of the grace of life, that your prayers may not be hindered.

It was this situation that allowed me to see that I was committing a sin by not honoring my marriage by putting myself, passions and goals first and not understanding that my husband had needs and that he and the kids came before all of that. It was through this pain that I was allowed to experience more deliverance and healing and start on the road to understanding the foundation of covenant and my role in it. I learned here at this moment that I had no other choice but to yield to God and surrender my marriage. During this process it was revealed to me that in order for our marriage to see a full manifestation of restoration and reconciliation that we had to acknowledge we had sinned against it and our covenant was no longer honorable in the sight of God. During this year God dealt with me one-on-one and showed me through the aid of the Holy Spirit how to be the change I wanted to see, and how to balance being a woman of God, wife and mother. I spent the next year journaling and allowing the Holy Spirit to lead me on the path that was designed for me.

I received strategies and wisdom that led to the road of reconciliation, stability and breakthrough in my marriage and with my children.

The rest of this book will target areas that I had to overcome and the strategies, declarations and prayers that were birthed during the process. I pray that you gain wisdom, guidance and direction towards your own personal breakthrough and restoration of your covenant.

FORGIVENESS

Mark 11:25 And whenever you stand praying, if you have anything against anyone, forgive him, that your Father in heaven may also forgive you your trespasses.

Reconciliation in a marriage will have to start with forgiving yourself and then forgiving your spouse. You will need to ask God to take you through healing and deliverance so that you can start the process of reconciliation. It is important and vital that you understand your individual wholeness before you can work on the wholeness of your marriage. If you stand on the word of God and activate your faith God will manifest and put your marriage and family back together. After you have begun the healing process and receive strength it is now time to expose the condition of your heart and your spouse's heart and release it to God to perform a spiritual heart transplant to remove any hardness or bitterness that has been rooted in hurt, rejection, or abandonment including infidelity and adultery.

Forgiveness removes the barrier that blocks you from breaking through, you have to look past all the hurt and damage and you cannot do this on your own this is why it is important to seek God in prayer for healing, deliverance and direction.

Zechariah 4:6

So he answered and said to me: "This is the word of the Lord to Zerubbabel: 'Not by might nor by power, but by My Spirit,' Says the Lord of hosts.

If you can't truly repent and forgive then you might as well not read any further because you have already blocked your restoration. You have to LOSE to win and forgiving others for hurt and pain they have caused you can sometimes feel like we are losing especially if your spouse is still manifesting the same behaviors that got your marriage to this place to begin with. Forgiving your spouse not only frees you up from the cycle of hurt and bondage in your marriage, but it gives God a chance to SHOW you the man in the MIRROR (yourself) so you can OWN (your part) then you can see that although your spouse has hurt you, you have to take responsibility for your part. Not taking responsibility for your spouse's part but making the focus about becoming the change you want to see. There are things you have done to accept, enable, and manifest these negative behaviors in your marriage, so it makes you just as guilty as them no matter what they have done. Note this book is based on my own experiences and I don't advocate any physical abuse in marriages, but I'm aware of the difficulty of being in a spiritually unbalanced marriage rooted in fear, mistrust, rejection and abandonment.

When I married I wasn't seeking God on my choice of a spouse and definitely wasn't even seeking God for any direction in my life. I say this because it is very important to know that just because we get delivered and set free, we feel that we are above our spouses spiritually. We feel it's okay to leave because we aren't yoked with this individual any longer. Well, I hate to be the bearer of bad news but this is not true and not a reason ordained by the word or God to leave a spouse.

2 Corinthians 6:14

Do not be unequally yoked together with unbelievers. For what fellowship has righteousness with lawlessness? And what communion has light with darkness?

The particular passage of scripture is not even talking about marriage. It's talking about light and darkness, believers and unbelievers. Just because your spouse does not pray like you, read the bible as much as you do doesn't make them lawless or part of the kingdom of darkness. Your spouse may be in a state of being a backslider, but an unbeliever denies Jesus and carries the spirit of the anti-Christ. When you married your spouse did you both believe? Being yoked with one who doesn't believe keeps you in a constant state of warfare and unnecessary bondage. If you both were unbelievers from the beginning and one receives salvation, you have to let the unbelieving spouse leave on their own accord.

I challenge you to go read all scriptures concerning marriage and allow the Lord to speak to you concerning your marriage.

Forgiveness Decrees

I declare that I have written down the vision and purpose of marriage and my life as it applies to kingdom living and principles of the word of GOD. I declare that the vision for my marriage will live and not die and that I will reap the reward of abundant life here on earth because I fainted not.

I declare that my heart and my spouse's heart are encouraged and strengthened in the Lord and we are being knitted together by the word of God and that we will fully understand the mystery and fullness of the father that we would attain all riches and glory as it is in heaven on earth

I declare that my spouse and I will find favor and blessings from the Lord because we are in covenant based on principles of the Word of God and forever practice forgiveness

Prayer

Lord I humble myself and lay prostrate before you praying, seeking and asking you for guidance. I repent of any sinful acts that would cause me to harm or damage my spouse, children, or family. I forgive myself, my spouse and anyone who has influenced me negatively to act out in my emotions and cause me to create a gap in our hedge of protection and a breech in our spiritual covering by acting in forgiveness. I pray that strategies are released that I may be equipped to walk in forgiveness fully for all the days of my marriage in Jesus name

Amen

FAITH

Hebrews 11:1 Now faith is the substance of things hoped for, the evidence of things not seen.

Let's take a look at our faith and ask a hard question. Do you have faith when it comes to your marriage? Well to be honest I have not always had faith in mine. I have asked myself many times why do I stay, is this ever going to get better, and just plain out right I can't do this any longer. I have wanted to throw in the towel so many times, but the God that is in me just wouldn't allow it. When God begin to deal with me and my faith and what my belief system was actually built on, well I got to see myself once again in a position of loss of hope, loss of faith and operating out of unbelief. It is here when I decided enough is enough and I would have to just trust what God is telling me and just step out on faith and believe that he would do everything that he said he would do. I started praying and seeking God to expose every hidden area that was causing issues in my marriage and to give me tools and strategies on how to pray against things that was causing confusion. Every time I would doubt, I would go to prayer release the feelings that I was having to God and just let go. Having faith is believing in something while you don't actually have it or see it. Remember it didn't take three weeks to get to the place you are at in your marriage, but this book just may be the tool necessary to push you to hop on your road to victory and recovery in your marriage.

Faith is built upon your belief in Jesus, if you lack faith in the vision that God has shown you for your marriage then you lack faith in your belief in Jesus. Yes, I said it! You lacking faith in Jesus! If you have been given keys and have been shown a vision of full restoration, why not trust in it? It was at this moment in my faith that I realized that I needed to tackle unbelief and trust the God in me to manifest the vision that I was shown. That was a vision of the full manifestation of God's healing, deliverance and full restoration of my marriage. It is time that you rise up in the power and authority God has given you and stand immovable in the gift of faith for reconciliation of your marriage.

Now that you have forgiven yourself and your spouse it is time to activate your faith. Although things may not seem ok and you may not be speaking or even on the same page in your relationship or your spouse may be doing things out of the ordinary you can't go by what it looks like. You are in a war with the enemy for your marriage and at this point both parties can't be in bondage and someone has to rise up and fight. Faith is the evidence of things hoped for in the things you cannot see. Although your marriage seems to be falling apart right before your eyes it is not what it looks like. You have to be willing to lose to win meaning your faith is in God and not in your spouse.

Thinking outside the box and not limiting our God is the key. You have to gain strength and momentum through Jesus. There so many times in my marriage I was ready to call it quits and move on, but instead I stepped out on faith and wrote out a vision for my marriage and allowed the Holy Spirit to reveal to me what was missing from our foundation and what we needed from God to have a marriage based on kingdom principles and the word of God. In my heart I knew God could transform but I had to be open enough to God and the Holy Spirit to see it even if I could not see it manifesting in the natural.

Your spouse may or may not yield to God's chastisement so you have to be opened minded, and know unless God allows your spouse to walk out don't rush to the court house or to a lawyer to file for a divorce. If you keep your mind stayed on Jesus there is a peace that will allow you to stand immovable while things are shifting into place. This is the warfare that you must endure to see your marriage breakthrough. These are things that we may not want to hear but have to be open to. Our God can do anything but does give us free will and will not force us to follow truth of his word. You have to know you still have a vision for your marriage, the picture of a Godly spouse and if you faint not God will manifest through your spouse in the right season.

I'm an open -minded person and I don't believe in my heart that God would have you to be in covenant and held in bondage by an abusive person or a person that you are unequivocally balanced spiritually with, but we do need to realize that if we choose our spouse without seeking God and come into agreement spiritually unbalanced, it is not right or biblical to break covenant in a marriage unless you are truly directed by the Holy Spirit.

If they are given a chance to repent and they make the CHOICE not too then you don't have to be held in bondage to that person because it will create bitterness and opens the door to more demonic manifestations, curses and soul-ties on you and your children. But again leaving has to be instructed by God and not by feelings, emotions or advise from people or your spiritual leaders.

This type of warfare is not for those who do not have a personal relationship with Jesus. This is the time especially if infidelity is involved that you need to ask the Holy Spirit for direction. I found that when I got to this point and wanted to throw in the towel God would just not let it happen. It was hard and it hurt, but there was always a peace that would come over me when I would yield and be obedient to the word and it was this peace that would allow me to trust the process and hold on to the vision and have faith that God would do just what he said.

So be mindful and be obedient to the word of God and be fully led by the Holy Spirit before making any life altering decisions. Once you have released your marriage to the Lord watch for heavenly doors to open and demonic doors to close. Do more watching, listening and praying over running your mouth. Stay silent and allow God to do the work. Remember God does not require our help for our hope is in him.

Faith Declaration

I decree that every hidden sin in my marriage is exposed so that faith can be activated to manifest restoration and breakthrough in my marriage

I decree that I will not waver on my decision to fight for my marriage but will stand firm on my faith that total restoration is here

I decree that God loves us so much that he sent his son to die that we could live in total freedom through salvation through Jesus

I decree that I have asked for reconciliation in my marriage and I have received it in Jesus name

I decree that my faith even as small as a mustard seed will remove every mountain in my marriage

I decree that every device, scheme, plot and attack against my marriage is thrown into the sea and restoration and healing is released now in Jesus name

I decree that I have no doubt that my marriage is fully restored

I decree that every step I make in marriage will be by faith

I decree that I have fought the good fight of faith to reconcile my marriage in Jesus name

Wives: I declare that I'm clothed with the beauty that God has imparted in the inside of me. My beauty is unfading with a gentle and quiet spirit. I declare I'm holy and beautiful in the sight of God and my husband. My husband trusts me and I accept his authority over our marriage and our household affairs at all times.

Wives: I declare that I'm a woman of submission. My husband is the prophet and king of our home. I repent of any disobedience to your word and I declare that I'm a woman of honor. I declare that it is by my actions and not my words that I win the heart of my husband. I bind up all fear and torment that the enemy may release making me feel like I'm inferior or less than to my husband. I release peace and trust in God that our marriage is moving according to the plans and purpose that God has designed for us.

Wives: I declare that my husband is blessed and rejoices in me he sees me as young beautiful woman even my aging body will satisfy him all the days of our lives and he will always be captivated and enraptured by my love.

Wives: I declare that my husband lives joyfully with me all the days of his life it is his duty to God to labor in Love for me.

Husbands: I decree that I will give honor to my wife all the days of my life, I will understand and love her just as God loves me. I will honor her strengths and not treat her as a weaker vessel but take gratitude in the fact that she balances our marriage and her part of the covenant is just as important as mine. I will take great honor in my wife, for the word of God says I'm blessed and highly favored because I honor her, my wife is a gift from you God.

Husbands: I declare that I understand that my wife was created for me to be a helpmate for it is not good for me to be alone

Husbands: I declare that I am the prophet, the king, and the headship over my marriage, wife, and children. It is my duty to protect, provide, and led my family to Jesus. Let our home be a place of love and security. The fruit of my labor is a family founded in truth.

I declare that we have entered into God's perfect peace and we shall have sweet rest in our home and as we lay and walk in uprightness and give glory to God.

I declare that two are better than one and we both understand that we need each other and we will be rewarded for our labor in love. We shall lift one another up especially when one is down.

Faith Prayer

Dear God I thank you in advance for the victory in my marriage. I give all glory and honor to you and I place my life and marriage in your hands. Lord activate a new level of faith and break all idolatry and demonic soul ties associated with demonic holds that are in my marriage. Create a new foundation a solid foundation where your son Jesus Christ is the cornerstone. I release faith and align myself with you God and I'm open and ready to receive. I thank you that you have elevated my faith to continue the journey of covenant. Thank you for providing me with the example of true covenant, for you have never broken covenant with me and I too will stand as Jesus would stand and endure to the end. I trust your word and your promises to fulfill, reconcile and strengthen my marriage even in times when things aren't going to well. Thank you Lord for activating my faith today and may each day get easier to stand and wait on your promises in Jesus name

Amen

Healing

Luke 9:11 But when the multitudes knew it, they followed Him; and He received them and spoke to them about the kingdom of God, and healed those who had need of healing

Healing is vital in reconciliation because it is part of your mental stability to not get into your feelings or go into emotional overload. This is often described as the soulish realm. Because we are made of a body, soul and spirit. Your emotions are manifested through the soulish realm. When you are healed in this area you have a greater chance of not having pity parties and being a crying victim. You will not waste time and energy on complaining about not being happy and not being satisfied in your marriage, but healing will shift you into a place of having more self-control so that you may go from a place of operating out of defeat to walking in a place of victory.

If you feel like crying please cry it is ok to be balanced in your emotions but it is dangerous to be controlled or moved by them. You may need to release to a close trusted friend about how you feel, but be careful not to turn it into a pity party or a spouse-bashing session to build you up. You may feel like family, work associates and people who are on the outside looking in are attacking you personally, so be mindful when sharing with people in the above categories. Most people in this category don't know about your personal life like they think they do and may be shocked or too judgmental to be able to give support without being bias.

I was reminded that you have to rely on what God has showed you people who have not been shown your restoration will oppose what God is trying to do in and through your marriage. Relying on an assumption is very dangerous and will prolong your spouse's deliverance and reconciliation of your marriage. I remember I was shown a vision of my husband's breakthrough and it wasn't until almost three years later before I even learned how to war over what I had been shown. I wasted a lot of time on idle talk and trying "explain" to him about how to get free instead of showing him how to be free. It took this long because I was being selfish and not listening and obeying the word of God. I was held captive by fear and still needed a measure of deliverance myself to even be able to endure the battle that I had before me. It wasn't until I decided to LET GO of the marriage in order to gain the marriage that I wanted and we both deserved. I had to command fear out of my marriage and my mind in order to take action to activate my faith and start healing, in order to even be ready for the blessing of a marriage created straight from the throne room of God you have to be healed.

The healing wasn't for my husband, although he desperately needed healing himself, but it was for me so that I could be able to nurse our marriage back to life. It was so I could guide and support him through his process. During healing it is when I learned why I had to be delivered before my spouse and it is through healing that I understand my role as a wife to cover my marriage, spouse and family in prayer.

Healing Decree

I declare today that I have been dipped in the pool of Bethesda and I'm receiving full and total healing so that I may be able to assist in the breakthrough of my spouse's true freedom in Jesus which will lead to a fully restored and reconciled marriage.

I declare that today I'm choosing to serve God, and my spouse and I will turn from the sins and generations curses and cycles that keep our marriage in bondage.

I declare that our home is peace, and we are secure in it, our family and marriage is blessed and we will find rest in it

I declare that my spouse understands that giving honor to the weaker vessel shows that we are heir's together living in the grace of life and that there is no block or hindrance in our prayers

I declare my spouse releases affection to me always and that I release affection to them as long as we are one.

35

I declare that I will submit to only my spouse and my spouse will submit to only me and we will love one another and will not harbor bitterness in our hearts toward one another

Healing Prayer

Lord I thank you for healing all our deep wounds and breaking generational curses. I understand that although my spouse has hurt me, I have forgiven him in order to reconcile. I thank you for breaking generational cycles in my life, healing me and giving me the wisdom and guidance to know when and how to draw from the pool of Bethesda so that I may support my spouse in healing and breakthrough so that they may experience the fullness of true freedom in Jesus. It is here at the pool of Bethesda, Lord where many healings took place. I ask you Lord to heal and restore our marriage today. That we may rise up and take authority over the pain and suffering and walk it out and testify to the world that you God are still working miracles on behalf of your people and marriages even in the present day. In Jesus name

Amen

Understanding Headship

1 Corinthians 11:2-3 2 Now I praise you, brethren, that you remember me in all things and keep the traditions just as I delivered them to you. 3 But I want you to know that the head of every man is Christ, the head of woman is man, and the head of Christ is God.

During my reconciliation process I was consumed by the definition of what it means to have a "head" of the house. By biblical terms the husband is the head or leadership of the marriage. Although the wife is not the head, understanding the role of the head and how to respond to the authority makes a difference on how successful your communication can be in your marriage. We make the mistake of getting married and not truly understanding what our role is as a wife or husband and respond based off our emotions instead of responding the way Jesus would have us respond.

Our spouses may or may not understand their role as head and doesn't walk as Jesus would lead but they lead based off what they have learned or watched a father do or has no clue at all because there was not a male role model in the home growing up to begin with. These are things that are important to know before going into covenant. It is very important to know generationally where your spouse comes from.

Usually in a case of spiritually unbalanced marriages neither party understood their role in the first place. It is not until the veil is removed and one of the two receives deliverance that the true manifestation of Kingdom covenant can take place in your marriage. This is why it is so important to study the word of God and understand each role and perform the expectations of your role according to the word of God, receive counsel, and deliverance before getting married. When seeking counseling, if possible seek counsel from someone who is rooted in the word of God.

In my case when I got married we already had children and had lived together, we both believed in Jesus but lived in double mindedness when it came to being obedient to the word of God. I look back at it now and realize that we made so many poor choices and lack of knowledge and the understanding of biblical marriage led to our demise. Being in bondage and then creating a marriage out of captivity produces more bondage and greater problems. You see when you look at it from this point of view you see the "TRUTH" for what it is.

The Holy Spirit revealed to me what role the "HEAD" was and what my responsibility to my headship was. Jesus expects for your husband to be your covering, without a husband God is your covering just as he covers his son. A husband should take great pride in God allowing him to cover you as his wife and you should be grateful and praise God that you are blessed enough to have a headship. The husband's role is not to make you a slave, but to cover and rule over you as his equal. He is to lead you with love and treat you the way that he would want to be treated. The head should never push your buttons or purposely provoke you to anger. (Example: picking fights or arguments just to get a RISE out of you.)

A husband should lead by example so that his sons and daughters aren't cursed by his sins. The husband should always keep in mind that he is being watched by God and will be judged according to his actions. Wives must you learn your husband's ways. It is wise that we use wisdom on how we respond to their behavior whether it is positive or negative. In my situation I realized that although my husband did some things that caused me a lot of emotional pain, stress, and mental triggers to my past trauma, most of it was because I didn't know how to fight in the spirit and I wasn't equipped to handle having a head that wasn't led exclusively by the word of God.

I realized that I was actually blocking his deliverance and hindering him from total breakthrough because my responses were keeping the door to his healing and deliverance closed. I wanted to teach him on how to be free and delivered instead of letting him experience the same pain and loss through the process that would lead to his breakthrough. I was reminded of how depression led to me nearly losing my husband and children. And then opened the door to me wanting to commit suicide and eventually led to my own healing and

38

deliverance. When I thought about that, this is when the light bulb went off and it was time for me to step back. When I released my husband to God and started allowing God to strengthen me as a wife I started to see some positive manifestations. I started to actually see some of things that God had been trying to show me in the past, but because of lack of patience and selfishness my marriage stayed bound in areas that could have been free sooner.

In a perfect world we would know all of this beforehand and have the happily ever after, but what glory would God get if we didn't have to fight, sacrifice, or suffer a little. I learned you have to be unlearned to learn and you have to lose to win. Anything worth having is worth losing and anything worth winning is worth a sacrifice. The bible talks about strength, perseverance, and suffering, taking up crosses and bearing burdens. Why would God have put all of this in the bible if we weren't to experience it? These trials and tests are purposed for our destinies and abundant life on earth. Yes, our eternal award is to be with the father but God did promise through his son abundance on earth.

John 10:10 The thief does not come except to steal, and to kill, and to destroy. I have come that they may have life, and that they may have it more abundantly.

So wives and husbands realize that God delivered you to give you the keys to be able to support your spouse through their process, and if done correctly you will start to see God's power manifest over your marriage. You have to be able to completely hear the Lord's voice and be led completely by the Holy Spirit. You will have to learn how to pray and release to God during this time because an emotional response to your spouse will just cause a setback and a block to the door of reconciliation. If you go back and think about your own salvation, healing and deliverance, it didn't happen overnight and you will continue to be delivered and processed until God calls you home.

This is the KEY. Kingdom is not a phase; it is a total lifestyle change and you have to CHOOSE it on your own. But keep in mind that everyone doesn't make the choice to be free. So always be willing to lose to win.

Headship Decree

I declare that my headship has separated from his father and mother to become one with me his wife.

I declare that my headship and I are one flesh and what God has put together no one or thing can separate us.

I declare that my headship has put away his childish mindset and has become a man.

I declare that my headship fears the Lord and takes great pleasure in doing what is pleasing in God's sight.

I declare that my headship flees from his sins and pursues righteousness, Godliness, faith, love and patience.

I declare that the wicked part of my headship is dead, the enemy will perish and all schemes, plots, and devices are broken.

Headship Prayer

Prayer: Thank you Lord for imparting wisdom to me about my headship. Lord grant me the tools and strength to fight for my covering. Allow me to see and honor the headship you have blessed me with. Download tools and keys so that I may become a support system to aid my headship in deliverance and healing instead of being a hindrance. Release wisdom on his ways and how to respond to all his behaviors properly whether it is positive or negative. Today I stand for kingdom principles and I will aid in the intercession for the head of my home and children. I break all assignments plots and schemes that the enemy would try to release for releasing this prayer and I release the power of the blood that conquers all things and seal this prayer with it in Jesus name.

Amen

It's a Process

Proverbs 3:5 Trust in the Lord with all your heart,
And lean not on your own understanding

You hear "trust the process", which is said by many who want to see your breakthrough. With my experience with the process I never understood what it meant. I needed a NOW revelation, but was only getting an endpoint explanation. I wanted to know why; I had to trust the process and what steps I would need to take in order to shift in the right direction. When you hear the word process you need to expect to experience constant change, change in jobs, change in ministry, change in relationships. Change will not always feel good but it will be good for you. When you are being processed you will go through cycles or series of different events that will teach and train you. The process is intended for you to learn what is on the inside of you so that you may fulfill your purpose; this includes pioneering reconciliation in your marriage.

Once your process starts, you will not be able to turn back even if you may fall short or want to give up. At times you may feel some stagnation or a standstill but if you try to go back it won't be comfortable at all. When you realize that you are being processed, you will start to see and feel changes. Some may see or feel things sooner or later than others. Your process has been ordained by God to be uniquely designed for your destiny and purpose so it won't always look the same as someone else. So you can't discredit someone else's experiences based on your own and should be always led by the spirit when imparting or supporting someone through theirs. I found personally during my process that each season God was focusing on different aspects of my marriage, personal life, my purpose, call and destiny all at once. Some may experience lots of healing for a season, and then you may have a season of breakthrough, favor and blessings. When you start to shift through different seasons you may experience the physical effects to your natural body and mind. You may feel fatigue (tiredness), sadness, extreme joy or sadness and can't explain why. This is a time to get in your word or call someone to pray. I learned that these symptoms help you learn how to understand how your discernment works also.

41

It could be other symptoms for others but these are the ones that I experienced myself. When you start to feel, then it is time to go into prayer and seek God for what needs to be revealed to you in the current season. You can't go off just the emotion, the emotion of sadness may not be about you but it could be something that God is trying to heal you from that caused sadness in the past, or hurt from your relationship.

I believe that process is intended for God to see how far you are willing to go and to see how much more he can extend to you. With great power comes great responsibility. Some may have it lighter than others, but we are all seen through the eyes of God the same. We are one body but with different parts. So the process for one part to another may different but we are all important. You strive for holiness and righteousness and you may find that sometimes you just aren't capable and this is ok but not a free ride to engage in sin or turn away from the truth and it doesn't mean that God won't continue to love you. But you have to know that many people in this world have died and didn't get to experience the intended purpose why God truly placed them on the earth.

Marriage is difficult and not easy and I do believe that many marriages don't get to its full potential because of the hardships that follow it. The verse says many are called but only a few are chosen. When you accept your process it's a choice, God gives us freewill to choose but God won't love us less if we don't fulfill it. The process is the journey you take to get to the place where God has called you to be. God needs to know if you can be trusted with the mission, before you can get the full scope of things.

As long as you walk on this earth and you are living for God you will be going through the process not just in marriage but life. As God reveals keys to you, you will be able to pass the test a lot easier and move through the process with more confidence and power than you did when you first started. You will start to recognize the growth in areas when in the beginning you couldn't. As you continue in the process you will grow closer to GOD and rely more on God for help than yourself or others.

Remember the process started because you answered the call. When you accept the call, you are accepting what God wants for your life and your marriage. You cried out for help and God answered you, now it's time to surrender to the call.

Mark 3:13 ¹³ And He went up on the mountain and called to Him Those He Himself wanted. And they came to Him

I can speak from only my experiences and don't argue that there is more insight. When we are being processed according to biblical truth, we reap the rewards of the truth and when are processed through curses, sin, and demonic cycles, we reap the negative effects of this process. Often it is not until we are delivered that we have to become unlearned to actually learn how to operate the way God intended for us to operate for spouses, our children and ourselves. I can use myself as an example. I was raised in a single-parent home, however my mom eventually got married to an emotionally abusive man and stayed for 14 years. I was the victim of sexual abuse by more than one family member, and I fell into bondage because of cycles of abuse throughout my childhood that manifested in my adult life. Thank GOD for deliverance; for without it, I would still be held in bondage.

When I got married we were both wearing blinders and were not open to biblical truths especially when it came to marriage and family. I most certainly didn't have self-worth, self-confidence, self-identify, self-control and many other areas that remained locked at the time of my marriage. It would be almost 7 years later after healing and deliverance and becoming unlearned that I realized that my marriage never stood a chance without the blessing and favor of GOD. Meaning Jesus had to be the cornerstone. I remember sitting in our apartment about 4 years prior to birthing this book and heard a jackhammer outside, so I looked out the back patio and noticed that the apartment complex hired a contractor to break up the foundation all around the pool. The Holy Spirit spoke to me as I was looking at this and said the foundation in your marriage is being broken up so that a new one can be poured. At first I was like YES!!! Until all hell started to break loose and the fight for my marriage really commenced. The warfare was so heavy and the test and trials seem never ending. The more I got free, the more my marriage seemed to decline. I thought, "OK? Am I really supposed to be fighting like this, am I fighting right?" Honestly I had NO clue what I was doing and a lot of time I was making matters worse, because I didn't know where I was in MY OWN personal deliverance and process, let alone fighting for my spouse and my marriage. I was a total wreck. This is when I learned I was actually dual processing, I was getting prepared, going through self-deliverance, deliverance and reconciliation of my marriage at the same time.

I learned so many things about myself and why I reacted to certain things and what made me tick. It was here where I learned to fight the unseen enemy rather than fight my husband and be full of emotions and opening doors for the enemy to gain ground in my marriage. After I learned how this process actually worked, it was easier for me just to allow God to do the work and for me to just rest in him. It was at this point I realized that I could journal through my pain and help someone else not to have to fight with a veil on. It was during this journey that I realized my breaking was for another's breakthrough, the deception I was fighting was for another's deliverance and the hindrances I faced was for another's healing. I wasn't confident in myself and I didn't know what my purpose was. I was deceived because when we married we were evenly yoked; I repeat we were equal in our beliefs. We shared the same beliefs and views on believing. After my deliverance and breakthrough for the first time I started to see the truth for what it was and it hurt so badly. I couldn't believe how much emotional damage I allowed to happen to myself.

I say I allowed it because I did, I didn't have the courage to even stand up for myself, and I allowed people including my spouse to have me living in fear and feeling like a failure. I wasn't prepared to be a wife; I hadn't even learned how to be a woman. Although I thought I had it going on I knew nothing. You must know that you will process your entire life in the areas of self-growth, growing in marriage and growing as a parent, co-worker, friend, leader etc. We will never stop processing whether it be good or bad you will process.

The process is a course and you have to be able to hear from GOD to understand where you are and what season God has you in at the time and when and how you are being processed. If you are allowing God to order your steps and you are walking in obedience to the promptings of God you will absolutely see a manifestation of God's glory, healing, deliverance, miracles, signs, wonders and breakthrough will be all around you.

Demonic doors will shut and heavenly doors to your marriage and life will open. As time goes on even if you haven't received a full manifestation of reconciliation, even when things look bad you will begin to seek God on what is going on and how you need to react. Sometimes you will need to pray and fast, other times you will need to decree the word. You may have to speak the word of God to block and hinder the movement of the enemy and yet sometimes God will just want you to put away your boxing gloves and just rest. When you are at this level you will be able to rest in God and be in peace no matter what it looks like. This is so important during the time of reconciliation because so much is going on in the natural if you aren't in the spirit it is easy to get caught up in your emotions and flesh. You will need to draw strength from the word of God and spend quiet time with God. If you allow your flesh to take over it will lead to confusion and defeat. Sometimes you will want to throw in the towel and part ways with your spouse. Believe me I fought this feeling many times throughout my process. Being in the process of reconciliation will require you to prepare, perform various tasks, and stand in your faith. God determines the true time frame and will terminate each stage of the process when you are ready to transition to the next. The more you trust God, the more God can trust you with more. Meaning more territory, greater in marriage, family and life. Your greatest and most powerful ministry will be to be a great steward over your marriage and family.

Process Decree

I declare that I will continue to press through to the reconciliation of my marriage. I will release past hurt and pain. I will continue to lean forward to the things that are ahead, I declare that I have a mind of Jesus and my marriage will be a blue print and pattern and example of what God intended for marriages and families.

I declare that I am chosen by you God and appointed to do your will concerning my marriage. I ask that you bless me and show favor to me and my spouse by giving us full reconciliation and restoration in our marriage.

I declare that I am blessed, I have endured the temptation and will await to receive the crown of life for the love I have shown to my Lord.

I declare that I walk in biblical truth and my marriage and family is an example for others to follow.

I declare that I'm not fighting a battle with my spouse but a battle with unseen enemies in heavenly places.

I declare that I am not in the flesh but I will walk in the spirit daily to be connected and obedient to my father in Heaven.

I declare that my boldness in Jesus will attract others to have faith and confidence in the Lord to save their marriages and families.

I declare that I will be at peace when it comes time for God to judge for through the misery of man he increases greatly.

I declare that I will never overcome through evil but I overcome evil with good.

Process Prayer

Lord I thank you for processing me and trusting me with your marital covenant. I thank you for wisdom concerning the process of reconciliation and I ask you Lord to forgive me for any selfishness and or lack in the area concerning my duties as a spouse. Lord I understand that this is a process and everything will work together for our good. Give me directions as I move forward and a discerning of the times to know what season we are in our restoration so that I won't act out in my emotions or in the flesh in Jesus name.

Amen

Perseverance

Galatians 6:9 ⁹ And let us not grow weary while doing good, for in due season we shall reap if we do not lose heart.

After you realize what part of the process you are in, it will be important to learn how to persevere. You will need to use the tools and gifts of the spirit to be able to stand even in the midst of difficulties. When the adversary is aware that you are getting insight and knowledge on truth and how to stand. You may see some difficulties and be thrown into some obstacles that you will have to stay in a state of GRACE to the end.

I found that I had to be immovable and stand no matter what or how I was being shifted. You cannot be easily pulled asunder when you are restoring any type of relationship especially a marriage. The key to perseverance is knowing your opponent is not your spouse, but a demonic spirit that comes to kill, steal and destroy. When these different spirits begin to manifest in your spouse, it is a time to go into prayer and warfare using the word of God. You will have to be disciplined and be led by the spirit during times like this. You have to be careful also, not to think that you, meaning yourself, can't be used by the enemy. When we create doors even small ones the enemy will try to come in and will come in like a flood! And use you to create confusion and chaos in the midst of restoration. So it's time to fight with the word of GOD and not with words of emotions and pain.

When you start to fight in the spirit and you are gaining momentum and learning your jurisdiction in the spirit you then will begin to see change. If you are not seeing any visible changes, it is not because God is not working; a lot of work is done in the realm of the spirit where we can't see what is going on. But you can pray to God and seek for answers on what may be happening. You must realize that if you are in a war for your marriage and you too are getting processed there may be something for you to learn that may be causing the delay. It is very important to keep in mind that this is not a blame game and you should be learning and sensing what your responsibility is to this marriage and that it takes two to tear it up.

You can't blame it all on your spouse. Own your part and yield to your own healing and deliverance that way you can preserve and gain strength to continue on. You may not understand everything that is going on but you just have to keep moving forward. It will get harder and harder as you continue to press through but don't give up and don't lose hope just keeping going and remain in the faith. If any part of your marriage is worth keeping, then it is worth fighting for.

Perseverance Decree

I declare that I am steadfast and immovable and staying the course until I see a total manifestation of reconciliation in my marriage.

I declare that I will not grow tired and weary while I'm waiting on the Lord to move on my behalf for the restoration of my marriage. My heart grounded in the word of God and I shall reap the benefits of standing and trusting in it.

I declare that I am blessed and have been refined through test, trial, temptations and tribulations, I love the Lord and gain the promises for my marriage and family for my obedience to the word of God

I declare that I am sustained by the grace of God and my suffering will establish strength and peace in my marriage and family

I declare that my marriage sufferings are only for a short moment and the weight of eternal glory will exceed the pain and trials. I declare that my marriage will rise and is restored

I declare that my marriage will receive supernatural restoration because I'm patient in continually seeking God, his glory and his honor

I declare that patience is forever at work in my marriage for with it we receive complete restoration and manifestation of kingdom covenant lacking in nothing.

I declare that my spouse receives true witness from my actions and words and that their soul will receive healing and deliverance.

Perseverance Prayer

Lord I thank you for wisdom concerning perseverance; I understand that I must stay the course and allow you to continue to restore my marriage. Lord release strength that I may rise up and not faint during this difficult time in my marriage. Give me more understanding on my enemy and how to boldly come against the attacks with the word of God. I will be tenacious and immovable. Thank you for continued grace to the end that I will see a total manifestation of reconciliation in my marriage in Jesus name.

Amen

Deception

Matthew 16:23 *²³ But He turned and said to Peter, "Get behind Me, Satan! You are an offense to Me, for you are not mindful of the things of God, but the things of men.*

While you are continuing on this journey to reconciliation, there may be times that deception has found its way in the door causing you to get off of track and become distracted. Remember while reconciling your marriage the enemy is looking to derail you and get you heading in the wrong direction. You will need to know how to use the word of God to fight in an offensive way.

Deception will often try to manifest through the actions and words spoken toward you through your spouse and sometimes even your children. If not dealt with properly, this could set your breakthrough back or make it become stagnant depending on how much damage is done. More healing and deliverance may need to take place to continue on the path. Deception will have you to think that your perception of situations in your marriage that seem negative in the natural to be the full reality and this is not true at all, if you are patient and don't react right away God will reveal the truth about the situation and why it was allowed to even manifest in such a way to begin with.

I found that in my own marriage that when I stepped back and allowed God to reveal things to me, things that I would have reacted quite emotional to, because I listened to the voice of the Holy Spirit, I didn't react and saw what God was trying to reveal so that I could pray. It could be something as small as an awkward dirty look all the way to infidelity and yes I'm saying that the enemy will use infidelity to cause deception and distraction. Everything that we perceive with our own minds without insight through the Holy Spirit is built on fallow ground and is not always able to stand. But if you are seeing things one way and GOD is telling you that it isn't what it seems, although what you see often looks solid, it may not be the reality. I'm not saying that if you find your spouse in a bed committing adultery that it isn't what it looks like, of course it is. What I'm trying to say is that if GOD has given you a vision and a promise of restoration in your marriage no MATTER what comes up you have to TRUST in the vision and allow GOD to do the work. God speaks to all of us differently and we all are held accountable to our own obedience. I had to learn that I couldn't lean to my own understanding of what God was doing and I couldn't get advice from people looking on the outside of the situation.

A lot of my direction and movement came from releasing my frustration and anger out in prayer. I then would receive instructions on what to expect next. This put me in a position to be able to fight offensively, when in the past I struggled always fighting defensively. Sometimes fighting when GOD only wanted me to rest. The whole objective of the use of deception is to deceive you in deceiving yourself and changing the way you think or look at a circumstance that arises. When you are being deceived you "act out" on emotions instead of using the word of GOD, prayer, fasting, praise and worship. So now your flesh creates open doors to more serious attacks that could lead to giving up or throwing in the towel.

This is where I think a lot of divorces take place because people tend to get in their feelings mind racing with thoughts, there is no going back and making up for all of the hurt, pain and years of mess they have created. This is where the enemy steals, but I'm here to tell you when you feel like this you don't have to give up. There is someone out there ready and waiting to intercede on your behalf, there is someone assigned to your marriage with a greater anointing, wisdom, power and authority to break and cancel these demonic schemes, assaults, and attacks against your marriage and that is our father in Heaven. God may directly break the plans of the enemy or send someone in the natural to intercede; you may know or never know who is assigned to intercede on behalf of your marriage. The key is to stay in an offensive mode of fighting; this will require you to go into the enemy camp and spoil the goods. You will have to attack with the sword of the Lord and gain the ability to be ahead of the deception and distractions. You want to stay away from defensive fighting because it will mentally and physically wear you out if you aren't equipped and trained to fight from this position for long periods of time. The enemy likes to keep you in this fighting position because people tend to give up, and you become drained and spiritual awareness tends to be stagnant. You are constantly in PROTECT zone and don't have a lot of time to rest and be in a position for elevation and progress in the restoration. You become wounded more easily when fighting defensively; offensively there is little chance for wounds because your war plans have been given from God and God has given you the keys, coverage and protection needed to come out of the battle unharmed. You have to know that there will be deception and distractions, but fight them off with the word of God and keep your spiritual ears and eyes open for the strategies that God is trying to download to you.

Decree Against Deception

I declare that the strategic prayers being prayed against deceptions will release healing and restoration to my marriage in Jesus name.

I declare that love and the mercy from our God will preserve me and my marriage.

I declare that truth and wisdom remains my portion all the days of my life.

I declare that I won't be deceived by distractions or perceptions of my own flesh and desires.

I declare that the light of the truth shall prevail throughout my marriage and darkness be exposed that light may heal and restore my marriage.

I declare that my spouse and I are in unity and we will no longer be deceived by lies, schemes or plots of the enemy.

I declare that I am led by the spirit of truth and all doors to deception are closed.

I declare that my spouse and I walk in humility and we will be able to be held accountable for our actions that will led to repentance.

I declare that my marriage is founded on TRUTH.

Deception Breaking Prayer

Lord I receive the keys to the reconciliation of my marriage. I bind all deception and distractions and I break the power that has been released over my marriage and family in Jesus name. I release the blood to consume all things that are attacking my marriage and I release healing and deliverance to myself and spouse that past wounds and hurts are healed and we are delivered from the curses and cycles that come with the door of deception being opened in our marriage. Lord release divine strategies on how to fight offensively and stop the cycle of defensive fighting in Jesus name. I bind every assignment and plot of destruction placed in my marriage that would lead to divorce and I release the blood to consume in Jesus name. Lord I thank you in advance for your extended grace and strength to continue on the journey in Jesus name
Amen

Don't be offended

Luke 17:1 Then He said to the disciples, "It is impossible that no offenses should come, but woe to him through whom they do come."

When you feel hurt, violated or displeased by negative words spoken or actions by another you have just become the victim of offense. When we become offended by our spouses left unresolved, can lead to doors of bitterness, anger, and resentment being opened. This attack can happen all at once or over time. The key is not reacting out of your flesh or emotions the moment you hear or see something that has brought offense. If you can just walk away and pray, do just that. But if you can't, try your best to remain silent.

The spirit of offense is waiting for you to respond out of your flesh, but God is waiting for you to surrender it. Begin to ask God on how you need to respond to your spouse at the time of the situation. Sometimes if you just take a step back and think before you respond, you will find that maybe it was just what you needed to hear or see to get more healing and deliverance in an area you have been struggling with. The "truth" hurts and it takes some realness to get totally free. Some things our spouses say or do may seem very cruel or rude at time, but if you look past the cruel and rudeness and allow God to speak to you through the negativity. You will begin to see truth.

The enemy uses offense to distract you from what you really need to see or hear. Example: During a really tough time financially I had to now ask my husband for money for things that in the past I just did on my own. I would ask and he would say let me look into it to make sure we had enough although I already knew he had it. He did this constantly and I begin to take offense, meaning I felt like he was using the fact that I had to ask him for things to "control" and make me feel small for needing to ask him for things. But that wasn't at all what was going on. I wasted so much time dreading every time I had to ask my spouse for something until one day I decided I'm going to pray and ask God why I feel this way and why is my husband responding in this fashion always saying let me see if he has it knowing he does. It was so annoying and although this seems small, I would dread asking him because of the anxiety I would feel. During prayer the Lord revealed to me that my husband wants to provide all things for me, but I'm too independent-minded and not dependent on him. He likes for me to "need" him and he likes to give to me. God revealed that my husband was creating opportunities for me to return to him to ask for things and this is why he was responding in this manner, by giving me the run around about the money so he can hear that I need him.

It all made sense because when I looked back at it there wasn't one time he said no unless we really didn't have it and it was rare. It was further revealed that when I had my own money that I never asked him for anything, and it was like I didn't need him. Although he paid the bills he wanted me to ask him for everything and wanted me to see that he wanted to provide ALL things for me not just the necessities. I was picking fights and being mad at nothing, but I was deceived in my own mind by offense. I can't stress enough how easily your emotions and reactions can set you back in your restoration process. It's better to go into prayer immediately, when we aren't sure the motive or actions of our spouses.

I used a light example because I have found that in marriage it is almost always the smaller things that lead us to divorce than the bigger things. These smaller things build up to being bigger things over time. This is why you see marriages ending after 25 plus years. Being attacked in any form brings a feeling of outrage where you begin to feel mental instability or confusion even if only for a short period of time. This is the spirit of offense trying to make a home in your mind. You are left feeling violated, hurt and wounded. I pray you will be more aware of this spirit and take authority over it by being slow to anger and begin to be led by God in your responses to your spouse.

Decree Against Offense

I declare that I'm gentle and forever extending grace to my spouse to keep unity   and peace in our home.

I declare that I will not take negative words spoken by my spouse to heart.

I declare that my spouse and I stay repentant and forgiving in our marriage.

I declare that I will not judge my spouse and my spouse will not judge me.

I declare there is no envy in my marriage we are two joined together to make one, all confusion and evil are consumed by the fire of God.

I declare that pride and lies are not permitted in my marriage.

I declare that I will not send offense because I'm being offended, I will not seek revenge on my spouse who have caused harm and suffering, I will forever lean on the word of God.

I declare that I will tell my spouse with love how they have brought offense.

I decree that I'm slow to anger.

I declare that neither myself nor my spouse will bring offense to one another.

I declare that my husband and I have guards over our mouths and the door of our lips are protected by the blood of Jesus.

Prayer Against Offense

Prayer: Thank you Lord for exposing the spirit of offense. Give me the strength needed not to walk in offense in Jesus name. Allow me to be sensible and control my temper. Lord I will not take offense by my spouse's actions or words but I will love my spouse as I love me self. I take hold of every thought that would exalt itself above you Lord or what your word says. The spirit will lead me at all times and joy and peace is my portion in
Jesus
Amen

Rest

Matthew 11:28 Come to Me, all you who labor and are heavy laden, and I will give you rest.

Today we will reflect on how and why it is important to rest in God. So many times people would tell me just rest in God but honestly I would walk away and not quite understand what they meant I would think ok? Do I stop praying, fasting, praising and worshipping? Or do I just try to sleep for a few days. And the answer to both of those questions is no. There is a freedom when you choose Jesus and this freedom opens you up to a rest that is given to those who believe.

When you enter into God's rest you are no longer worried, having anxiety, you are able to enjoy the simple things in life and you can be at peace and allow God to finish the work that has already begin to be started. You can be confident that as you are obedient to what God is telling you to do that action is taken place in the spirit realm to manifest breakthrough here on earth on your behalf. Take time to reflect how well you have rested in your marriage or have you worried and fought yourself tooth and nail on whether you want to stay or leave.

When you have surrendered your marriage to God you should be at peace no matter what it looks like or what it sounds like. God is in control, so take your hands off the wheel and allow God to manifest his power through your marriage by remaining in a state of rest. There is no need to preach to your spouse or give them ultimatums; it is a time for you to sit back and watch a miracle happen right before your eyes.

When I accepted the fact that I had no control over my spouse's actions and only could control myself, there was a weight that was lifted off of me. It was no longer my job to worry about the why, what, and when, but my only job was to be secure in my faith that I was trusting God to do the work no matter what it looked like or felt like. In my rest I'm allowed to laugh, have peace, have joy and remain with hope that restoration and reconciliation would soon manifest.

During rest I found myself in more worship, prayer and fasting than ever. It didn't stem from a place of desperation but from of place of confidence. I was confidently relying on God to do the work. I no longer stayed up worrying or having anxiety about what was going to happen next, I just rested in God knowing that no matter what happened, all things would work together for my good.

Enjoy your rest.

Rest Decree

I declare that I will seek God for rest and walk in rest daily.

I declare Lord while you are restoring my marriage I will dwell in the secret place where I will find rest and protection.

I declare that I have ceased all labor and I surrendered to you so that I may rest.

I declare that I wait silently for God to move on my behalf by resting in the word.

I declare that God presence is forever with me as I rest.

I declare that my home is peaceful and protected by God as I'm resting in the word.

Rest Prayer

I thank you and praise you for allowing me to rest in you Lord. I will confidently rely on you to provide all my needs of security and protection in Jesus name. Lord release me into the shadow of your wings and allow me to rest with you in the secret place
in Jesus name
Amen

Patience

James 1:2-4 *²My brethren, count it all joy when you fall into various trials, ³knowing that the testing of your faith produces patience. ⁴But let patience have its perfect work, that you may be perfect and complete, lacking nothing.*

Being patient means to accept, tolerate or suffer without getting angry or frustrated from a situation, task or person. I believe that in our journey in life, marriage and family you will have to embrace patience.

When you are patient in trials and tribulations what you are really saying is God I accept a delay in my breakthrough and I understand that it is not a denial. I have strength from the Lord that will allow me to be at peace and not be angry during times of suffering. During times of patience you may become weary or feel drained. People will begin to tell you and ask you "How long you plan on waiting?" especially if you are waiting on breakthrough in your marriage. Or how long are you going to put up with the behavior? God didn't intend for you to be unhappy etc. (These are a few things people may or may not say.)

These statements will test you and make you feel like you are being ran over by your spouse or taken for granted. During my personal experience, I had been waiting for almost four years since the time I had first started interceding for my marriage. I had to ask myself many times how long should I wait? Do I deserve this? Do I deserve better? But each time I was told by God to be patient and continue to stand. It is not easy to do but God will provide you with the strength to endure and preserve.

It was during this time that God revealed to me that my spouse was feeling the same about me! Wow here I was saying I deserve better and how long it was going to take for him to change and the feeling was mutual! Boy, was this was an eye opener for me and changed the way I felt because although I felt these things knowing that my spouse felt the exact same way about me made me look at the situation now through a different lens. For so long I looked through the lens of a victim and now I have to look at it from being a perpetrator.

Many times we deceive ourselves by becoming the victim when the truth is both parties are victims by the actions of each and the attacks that have been released by the enemy. No I'm not blaming all on the enemy but when you allow someone or something to have access to you, this is the result! I don't advocate blaming the devil on everything but the reality is we give the devil a foothold by our choices and if you think you are out there making ALL the right choices, then you're denying the truth that all have sinned and fallen short of the glory of the Lord. Meaning you opened the door.

I charge you to be patient and allow the Holy Spirit to expose to you why things are progressing in the time frame that you feel they should and what lessons are you needing to learn instead of trying to figure out how long you have to wait. This mindset will keep you struggling in your marriage eventually leading to throwing in the towel.

Patience Decree

I declare that I'm a Godly spouse and will be rooted in being led by the spirit and will remain steadfast and immovable while going through trials and tribulations.

I declare that I am patiently waiting on the Lord to restore and reconcile my marriage in Jesus name.

I declare that I have forgiven myself and my spouse, because the Lord forgives me. I'm not moved or offended by past or present hurts.

I declare that my temper is controlled and led by the Holy Spirit, I'm respected by my spouse for overlooking their faults.

I declare that the Holy Spirit is producing patience in me to give me strength and power to stand.

I declare that I will celebrate my spouse's salvation and freedom and forgive the actions towards our marriage and family that has affected me negatively.

I declare that I will wait patiently for the Lord to show favor and blessings towards my marriage. May it be fueled with the Glory of the Lord because our covenant is in right standing with you Lord.

I declare that my love is strong for my spouse and I will patiently wait on their deliverance.

I declare the vision for my marriage is not delayed and as I wait patiently it will surely manifest in God's proper timing.

Patience Prayer

Lord I thank you for giving me patience to endure this season in my petition for full restoration in my marriage. I trust you that you are leading and guiding me in the path of full and total breakthrough in my marriage. Let me be led and guided by the Holy Spirit in all my ways concerning my marriage. I thank you for your gift of patience in Jesus name.
Amen

Silence

God will sometimes call us to be silent also known as holding your peace, the silence can be for a number of reasons, I found in my personal process that God wanted to be alone with my spouse and didn't need the help from me. God wanted to deal with me and wanted to deal with my spouse one-on-one. So the communication between my spouse and I was breached. When God is performing a great work on our behalf, he wants us to remain silent for one's words have power and can change the outcome and speaking out of emotions or prematurely could open the door for fear or confusion to manifest.

While writing this particular chapter, I had recently had my tooth cut out and it had been 8 days since the surgery and I was still in pain. While writing this I realized that when I wasn't speaking that my mouth wasn't hurting, but when I would engage in idle talk and meaningless words would come out, my mouth would begin to hurt again. So on this particular day, I decided I'm not going to say another word and I will watch and see what God does.

God wanted me to be quiet so he could work. There is life and death in the tongue, and I was speaking a lot of words that were causing death and delays to my reconciliation. God would like to do the work for us, but what I find is we think that we have to put our hands in the situation when God is calling us to step back. You need to quiet yourself and no longer speak of the things that bother you and of what needs to be changed in your marriage.

God has heard your petition and wants to release the manifestation of restoration but your words are creating blockage. God wants to remove veils that have been covering you and your spouse's spiritual eyesight towards yourself and your marriage. You both may need more truth exposed and continuing to focus on all the problems will keep you from the truth. This is part of the reason why reconciliation can't manifest because the truth is covered up. What your truth may be will vary according to your relationship. It may be hidden feelings, infidelity, lies, generational, etc. God wants every area that has been hidden to be exposed. So silence will help bring some peace and order so that God may do the work.

Discord, chaos and confusion make it hard for the work to be done on our behalf. We get caught up in wanting a change but won't go to God to ask God to remove the disorder of our atmosphere or surroundings creating the issues to begin with.

Our silence can also prepare us for a pending war, battle, fight or storm. You are fighting for your marriage and God may need you to be quiet in order to release the strategy, so you are prepared. Or it may just be that God wants you to be quiet because the things that are proceeding out of your mouth are making things worse not better.

We focus so much on what the other has done and we don't spend enough time examining ourselves and looking in the mirror and being the best we can be through Jesus. We are trying to prove a point and get someone to change based on selfish reasons because we want our flesh satisfied. The Father is concerned about our spouse as well as us so we have to be mindful of that when dealing with issues of the heart.

God may require you to be silent to keep peace and order while reconstruction and reconciliation is taking place. It is important that you examine yourself and ask God to reveal to you when and where you can remain silent in this season.

Silence Decree

I declare that confusion doesn't exist in my marriage but peace and understanding in its place.

I declare that I will remain in silence and I will not be rebellious so that I can stand in the strength of the Lord while my marriage is reconciled.

I declare as I remain silent that the Lord shall rise up and fight for me.

I declare that I will hold my words in and not release destruction against my marriage with idle words. Lord reveal to me the error of my words and forgive me where I have caused harm, hurt or confusion

I decree that my silence is precious in your sight and that I remain steadfast and immovable as you reconcile and restore my marriage.

I declare that I will quietly rest in you Lord as you come against the schemes and devices plotted against my marriage.

Silence Prayer

Father, I thank you for calling me to silence. Download wisdom, knowledge and revelation to why you have called me for such a time as this. Let your will be done as it is in heaven here on earth. Let my silence allow for order, peace and joy to be released and let the power of my silence break the bondage that has been placed on my marriage. I thank you in advance that a complete work is being done because of my obedience to remain silent, I thank you and praise you in advance for the victory in Jesus name
Amen

Understanding Love

Ephesians 4:2 [2] with all lowliness and gentleness, with longsuffering, bearing with one another in love

Love can be defined in many ways but your basic understanding of the word love is an intense feeling of affection, meaning the deepest intimacy you can feel regarding a person, place or thing. I say this to add that we are not only capable of loving other people but we can tend to be in love with other things. Understanding love and how we love, can make a big difference on how we love and how we give love. Most people release love the way they have been given it and shown it growing up.

During my deliverance, I was shown how I loved based off what I thought I knew about love and boy was I surprised that I didn't know what love was at all. If you have two people who grew up in two different households and were not shown love or gave love in the same way, then you are going to have a lovely mess on your hands!!! When the Lord started showing me that I really didn't have an understanding on love, then everything started to make sense to me. I didn't know how to give love or receive it because I didn't recognize it. The Lord didn't reveal to me that my husband didn't love me or this is what your husband needs to change. But the Lord said this is what YOU need to change and understand.

I got to look at the man in the mirror once again! I'm like God every time I come to you to help my marriage and I start dumping all these things about my spouse on you, I get a download of myself. So I asked God what is it I need to know. So the Lord said, "Have you ever took the time to just step back and understand what it is you need and see if you are really getting it?" OK, so at this point I'm like maybe God didn't hear my prayers. I broke it down really good about my needs and what I needed in a spouse so I just need to pray that again? Right! The answer was wrong! I needed to sit down and go through the laundry list of requests and see if I was actually giving it and the answer was no.

Again, God was actually holding me accountable before convicting my spouse. So I went down the list and as I begin to go down the laundry list of the things he needs to change, I started to see that the way my spouse responded to some of the demands that I would try to put on him that he was actually in the same place I was in feeling unloved!

Immediately I felt bad and thought wow, here are two people in the same place but neither one of us can help each other because we have no clue how to do it. But what I did know was we both loved each other. Although I wasn't getting it like I thought I should have been, but the reality was I wasn't giving it either. I was getting love the way he was taught based on how he received it as a child. I started watching how he responded to his siblings, his parents, to our children and I began to take notes and compare it to how he responded to me. Some things were similar but in this assessment, I started to see why I was feeling the way I was feeling and instead of saying, "You aren't doing this or that." I begin to say, "I need this from you." The way he was shown love and the way I was shown was quite different, but it could work. At the end of the day, we both were raised by parents that loved us, and they showed it the way they knew how and that was ok. So I was not to keep saying you don't do this or do that, but start to give the things I wanted and ask for them instead of saying you do not.

If you want more hugs or kisses, why complain to a person and say you never hug me or you never kiss me. I would begin to let him know I needed him. So instead I would say give me a kiss or come over here and let me hug you. Because as long as he thought I didn't need him, there wasn't any reason from him to release anything to me, in his mind all was well. In my situation being a strong independent woman was a good thing and a bad thing because I was so strong, I blocked myself from receiving love. What I gave off was I don't need anything. I got this. In reality all it did was push my spouse farther and farther away.

There were times when I felt like there is no way we are ever going to reconnect and that we had drifted so far away that we were doomed.

I thank God that I didn't give up on myself or my spouse. I kept praying and staying in a place of forgiveness and humility.

See what most don't understand is the biggest part of reconciliation is about restoring and getting healing for yourself before you can heal together. I believe that if one steps out on faith, God will supernaturally pull the other one in. It takes time and it will be a process but it will be well worth it in the end.

Learning about how you and your spouse love, giving and receiving are important. For most who have blamed the other for all the shortcomings of the marriage this will be hard, but I pray as you have read you are getting the key to what God is speaking about marriage and it is NOT ABOUT YOU. We placed ourselves in covenant with another person and vowed to stay with them until death do us part.

Unconditional love is just that staying and loving a person in spite of their shortcomings or faults. Meaning just because you love someone doesn't mean that you are going to like them all the time or be happy with them all the time. It's learning how to lean on God to persevere through the hard times. So what you told God at your marriage vows was you can trust me to love this person just as you love me (unconditionally). This is why it is wise to allow God to choose our mates for us, I believe that God chose my mate but I also believe we were not in God's timing and we had many setbacks because we weren't allowing God at the time to order our lives, steps, or decisions.

So I dare you to take time today to research the way you love and compare it to what is going on in your own marriage; you may just get a strategy that will change the way you look at the way your spouse is loving you and shift your marriage back in the direction that God intended for it to be.

Love Decree

I declare that as God loves the world I shall too love my spouse, let our marriage not perish but be filled with everlasting love.

I declare that I will suffer for the name of love concerning my marriage, my love and my spouse's love for our marriage is kind. Our marriage does not envy or doesn't look to gratified self all pride and stubbornness is crushed in Jesus name. Let truth continue to be unveiled as we release love to one another. Let our love and marriage be an example to our children that they know the ways of the Lord concerning love and marriage. Let us be drenched in unconditional love, forgiveness, and grace toward one another until death do us part.

I declare that I will treat my spouse the way that I would want to be treated in all things.

I declare that I will not walk in fear but I will walk in love all the days of my life. For as I walk in love, all torment in my life and in marriage is dissolved and reconciliation and restoration is released in Jesus name.

Love Prayer

Lord, I thank you for your unconditional love, I thank you for your daily grace and the gift of repentance and forgiveness. Lord, teach me your ways of love and teach me the way that you would have me release love to my spouse. Give me the key to my spouse's heart so that I can guard and protect it. Lord, forgive me in all ways that my love not your love, my words not your words and my actions not your actions to my spouse have not been acceptable to you. Lord, download prayers, strategies, wisdom and knowledge that will allow for us to reconnect and reconcile. Lord, allow me to see the unique ways that my spouse shows love and give me the ability to receive it. Lord, come against all generational curses that would block breakthrough in our marriage and break them all now in the Name of Jesus. I thank you and praise you in advance for the release of Love in my marriage in Jesus name.

Amen

Grace

Ephesians 2:8-10 For by grace you have been saved through faith, and that not of yourselves; it is the gift of God, not of works, lest anyone should boast [10] For we are His workmanship, created in Christ Jesus for good works, which God prepared beforehand that we should walk in them.

Let's talk about grace and how to give grace during all seasons of marriage and not just the good times. When God started to deal with me in the area of grace and how it concerned my marriage, man it was an eye opener. I saw how selfish I had become and that I even let my own desires over power what was best for my spouse, marriage, and even family.

Grace showed me that although I was mistreated at times in my marriage and some of the incidents created emotional bondage, pain and depression from my spouse, I too had released the same bondage, pain, and depression myself. This caused an immediate conviction, and as I started to see how God had given me grace and had saved and kept me no matter what I had done, it was time for me to show my spouse the same type of grace.

Easier said than done!!! As soon as I started to give grace, my spouse would do something that would set me off. I would plead with God on how could treating someone with kindness, love and respect when they aren't giving it to you really work. God's reply was you didn't treat me with honor or respect when you lived in your sins, and I still released grace upon you. So once again it was back on me. I started to ask God to show me areas where I was shown grace and wasn't deserving of it at all. It was more than I could handle, but I prayed and told God I would do anything to see my marriage restored and if giving grace was part of it I would. To model grace means that you have to show or give a person something good when they aren't deserving of it. I had to be completely honest with myself and put away anything that I needed for myself. I tell you when I started to look past my spouse's faults, and stay in a place of humility and prayer, I started to see results. It didn't happen overnight but the more I gave grace, the more changes I saw and it even led to my spouse giving more grace to me. Today focus on ways you can give grace to your spouse and not react to behaviors or situations that would typically set you off or take you there. Rest in God knowing that grace does change things and will change your marriage. Release grace today.

Grace allowed for me to look more attractive and pleasing to my spouse. Grace demolished any feelings of anxiety awkward feelings between my spouse and me. Grace allowed for us to respect each other and be polite when without it we were selfish and rude to one another. Grace manifested in my marriage when it didn't deserve it at all; my marriage was not fit or in alignment with the word of God but we were extended grace anyway. Because of grace, our marriage was regenerated and sanctified by God. We were now on our way to a more desirable and favorable marriage that gave glory to God. It is time to release grace and although it may not seem fair or feel good, it is necessary and will build character and integrity in your marriage.

Grace Decree

I decree that my marriage is strong in spirit, filled with wisdom and full of grace.

I decree that it is grace that will restore my marriage and not by my own works.

I decree that my marriage is receiving more grace as we humble ourselves before the Lord.

I decree that my marriage is saved by faith through grace

I decree that I'm boldly approaching the throne of grace concerning my marriage.

I decree that grace is given to my spouse and our marriage in Jesus name.

I decree that my strength in God to extend grace is made perfect through the struggles in my marriage.

I decree that I will not show a difference and keep record of wrongdoings toward my spouse; I will freely give grace concerning my spouse.

I decree that my marriage is ran by grace and will show that power of God through divine blessings and favor shown.

Grace Prayer

Father God in the Name of Jesus, we ask that you impart to us more of your grace in Jesus name. More of the attractiveness of your spirit that is pleasant and polite, we ask that you give us the skills needed and assistance to move and be aligned up with you to walk upright in our purposes and destinies by your grace in Jesus name. We decree that we will be strong in wisdom and ever-consumed by your grace in Jesus name. May we move only by your grace and not by our own works, Lord release true humility to us in Jesus name, that we may receive more grace. We come in boldness and confidence to the throne of grace that we would obtain mercy and grace in our times of need. Lord we ask that you impart your grace to us according to the measure of Christ's gift. I decree that your grace is sufficient and your strength is made perfect in our weakness. We boast in our weakness and trials that your power will rest upon us in Jesus name. We bind the works of the flesh and release the power of the blood to break its power in Jesus name. For we have all sinned and have fallen short and are in need of your grace for righteousness sake. Let your divine blessings, favor, and power that are manifested through grace rest on us in Jesus name to do great wonders, signs, and miracles through your Holy Spirit. We thank you and give you praise in advance all glory and honor goes to you in Jesus name I pray

Amen

Sex and Intimacy

Hebrews 13:4 Marriage is honorable among all, and the bed undefiled; but fornicators and adulterers God will judged.

I believe this scripture tells us how honorable and respectful the marriage bed is and how if you really dig deep in the scripture you will find that it gets detailed of how powerful the sexual experience is when released in marriage. Song of Solomon gives a few examples:

Song of Solomon 1: 2-4 Let him kiss me with the kisses of his mouth For your[h] love is better than wine. [3] Because of the fragrance of your good ointments, Your name is ointment poured forth; Therefore the virgins love you.[4] Draw me away We will run after you; The king has brought me into his chambers. We will be glad and rejoice in you. We will remember your[i] love more than wine. Rightly do they love you?

This speaks so much. It tells me that we can kiss each other deeply and that my spouse's lips against mine are far better than even a glass of wine. It shows how the smell ignited passion. Think about what happens when a man or women walks by you and the smell of his cologne or the smell of a woman's perfume does something to you. God created these scents to purposely bring an attraction between a man and woman. Because of the attraction, this woman wanted to be taken away into a private chamber and have this man give himself to her.

This is why sex before marriage is forbidden, not because it's bad but because it is so powerful. I believe that as long as you are capable of having sex in your marriage, meaning there isn't anything preventing it such as medical reasons or something permanently has happened that a spouse can't perform, you need to be getting it on regularly.

Song of Solomon 2:4 I charge you, O daughters of Jerusalem, By the gazelles or by the does of the field, Do not stir up nor awaken love Until it pleases.

Our sexual encounters are to be private and intimate and are not to be disturbed or corrupted by other parties, meaning no extra people and acts of perversion. I don't want to list a marriage sex list of what you can do and what you can't do, but I urge you that if you have questionable things that you are uncomfortable with like a particular sex act, I urge you and your spouse to discuss this prior to engaging in the activity.

You may even find that because you have had sex with another prior to marriage that the soul-tie with those partners are preventing you from fully engaging with your spouse. A soul-tie is the spiritual connection that takes place between two people who engage in sexual relations or intimate relations sometimes known as emotional attachment. These relationships need to be dealt with and broken through prayer. Sometimes being sexually violated can cause blockage also. So it is very important to be as open with your spouse as possible. Getting healing and deliverance from sexual immorality, sexual abuse and fornication will open your bedroom to more pleasure than you could ever imagine.

The bible makes it clear to only spare sex when you are in times of separation for prayer and fasting and seeking guidance and this should only be for a short time.

1 Corinthians 7:5 ⁵ Do not deprive one another except with consent for a time, that you may give yourselves to fasting and prayer; and come together again so that Satan does not tempt you because of your lack of self-control.

God is very clear that sex is not a game and should not be used to trap people or used as a weapon to control or get what you want. So you can't just say we are separated or I need to pray and fast so we cannot have sex. All of these things must be done in agreement. If you decide that separation is necessary beware that you are opening a door of temptation if you both aren't seeking God for reconciliation or restoration. Even if you are ready to give up it is not a reason to engage in sexual activity with a partner outside of your marriage. I charge you to look deep into the scriptures and know that God created sex for us to multiply and recreate but he also designed it to be pleasurable. Sit back and write down something's you can do to bring the fire back into your bedroom.

Sex and Intimacy Decrees

I declare that I will honor my marital bed and forever satisfy my spouse sexually all the days of our marriage.

I declare that our sex life is private and held sacred between my spouse and I.

I declare that I will never use sex as a way to control my spouse and will always give myself freely to them.

I declare that I will always share my most intimate desires with my spouse; that they will continue to be pleasing in my sight and the sight of God.

I declare that we will use Godly judgment when engaging in sexual acts and that our bed is not defiled by sexual immorality.

Sex and Intimacy Prayer

Thank you Lord for providing wisdom and revelation concerning the marital bed. Keep our marital bed covered and protected by the blood of Jesus; let everything performed in our chamber be pleasing in your sight. I bind up all soul-ties that are creating blockage in our sex lives to be broken. In Jesus name and let the joy, pleasure and peace flow down from heaven that will provide us with tools to ever satisfy each other all the days of our lives.

Amen

Reflection

1 Corinthians 13:12 For now we see in a mirror, dimly, but then face to face. Now I know in part, but then I shall know just as I also am known.

Let us reflect on all that we have learned so far and all of the demolition that has taken place in our marriage. God reminded me that when you are remodeling a home you must demo or remove the older outdated stuff so that the updates can be put in to restore, upgrade and increase the value. God allowed a few things to be removed and now cleansing needs to take place before God can start to place the new things into your marriage. God has started the process because of the acts of forgiveness. Our faith activated and healing released has allowed God to remove veils of deception and offense so that truth may be received. We have learned about our headship and how we are to honor it. We have learned how to properly communicate and learn our spouse's behaviors whether positive or negative so that we can release love, grace and forgiveness to them.

We aren't to enable negative behavior but seek the Lord for wisdom on how to respond to it. There may be ups and downs on the emotional rollercoaster and that's ok, you will just have to stand on the vision that God has given you. Be mindful of those who said that they were FOR you but when the miracles are manifesting they start to speak curses against your reconciliation, be very careful whom you speak to about the process today because you might just end up hearing a negative response from someone that you thought supported you.

Understand that it is not flesh and blood that we fight against but it is spiritual powers that are unseen that raise up against us through people, usually ones that are very close to us. Make sure you keep an open mind and know that unless GOD puts his finger down, it is not going to happen overnight. (Although if God wanted to manifest that in your life, he could.). So today stay in the spirit, fast if you have to and gain strength and momentum to carry on. Continue to reflect, journal and learn more about your covenant and know that your marriage is a forever journey to becoming one.

Reflection Decree

I declare that my husband is sober, temperate, sound in faith, in love and in patience. I'm a wife of reverent behavior who does not slander others and teaches good things. I love my husband and teach others to do the same. I am a woman of discretion and I'm obedient to my husband the word of God is not mocked by my behaviors.

I declare that I will pray earnestly and will be watchful in prayer giving all glory and thanks to God.

I declare that I will watch and pray so that I won't be tempted nor my husband. My spirit is always willing but my flesh is weak. I will continue to consecrate my flesh and keep it under subjection.

I declare that I have forgiven my spouse for all hurt and harm so in turn my Father in heaven will forgive me also.

Reflection Prayer

Thank you Lord for reconciliation, healing, deliverance and wisdom. Continue to keep my marriage covered by the blood. I cancel all assignments schemes, plots, and devices of the enemy now in Jesus name and I break the power that is being released over my marriage. I release full restoration and a new foundation for it to be built on. Continue to give me perseverance and a forgiving heart. Let me not grow bitter and angry toward my spouse but allow me to learn their behaviors that I may respond in the way of Jesus. In Jesus name.

Amen

Journaling

Declaration: I declare that miracles are taking place in the heavens and are manifesting supernaturally on earth to create reconciliation and security in my marriage.

Journal Entry:

_____
_____
_____
_____
_____
_____
_____
_____
_____
_____
_____
_____
_____
_____
_____
_____
_____
_____
_____
_____
_____
_____
_____
_____
_____
_____

Declaration: I declare that I am a person of faith and I place my marriage, family and spouse in the hands of God. The right hand of God been released to turn my marriage into a covenant based on biblical principles.

Journal Entry:

_____
_____
_____
_____
_____
_____
_____
_____
_____
_____
_____
_____
_____
_____
_____
_____
_____
_____
_____
_____
_____
_____
_____
_____
_____

Personal Declaration:

Journal Entry:

_____
_____
_____
_____
_____
_____
_____
_____
_____
_____
_____
_____
_____
_____
_____
_____
_____
_____
_____
_____
_____
_____
_____
_____
_____
_____
_____
_____
_____
_____

Author's Remarks:

Congratulations! You have just opened the door to the process of restoration and reconciliation in your marriage. Remember to continue to fight the good fight of faith by praying and standing in your faith knowing that all things in God work together for the good of those who love him and have been called for his purpose. So if you have completed this book, you have been called to pioneer the reconciliation and restoration of your marriage.

Blessings and Favor,
Lateena

ABOUT THE AUTHOR

Lateena is a bold confident woman of God, wife of king and mother of 5 that has made it her passion to see breakthrough and freedom in her family by using the word of God as a foundation to create peace, stability and structure in her life and household. She demonstrates through the maturing of her life choices and adversities that she has overcome that there is freedom in accepting salvation through faith and grace by believing in the ministry of Jesus and applying the word of God to your life. It is her purpose to leave a legacy for generations after her and to set the captives free. When Lateena is not ministering the word of God she is busy balancing, marriage, children and her career. She enjoys family vacations and supporting her children in their sports and activities. Family is the foundation of her ministry and it is her passion to see families everywhere experience peace and freedom.

Contact Lateena : www.perazimempowerment.com
Email : perazimempowerment@gmail.com

Made in the USA
Monee, IL
15 March 2020